MY ARABiC COLORING BOOK

First Name: .... :الاسم

Last Name: .... :اللقب

ISAAC DESIGN

Important For Parents:

Sharing this book with your child is the ideal way to help him/her start the enjoyable journey of learning the Arabic Alphabet. This book will establish the skills needed for confident learning and will act as an invaluable prompt for reading and becoming familiar with Arabic letters and numbers.

Your child will enjoy browsing through the book, looking at the attractive illustrations, reading and coloring the Arabic letters and words. Every picture shows a cute animal labeled with its English word and then its Arabic word. This encourages an immediate association of Arabic words and animals so that young children can enjoy learning new Arabic words.

Chapter 01:

Let's Color The Arabic Alphabet With Cute Animals

Arnab	Alif	أ

أَرْنَب

Rabbit

Batta	Baa	ب

بطة

Duck

| Timsah | Taa | ث 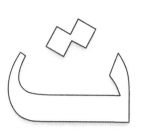 |

تمْساح

Crocodile

Thaeleb	Thaa	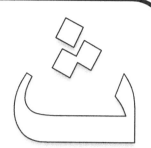 ﺙ

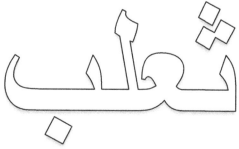
ثعلب

Fox

Jamel	Jeem	ج

جمل

Camel

| Hissan | Haa |  |

حصان

Horse

Kharuf	Khaa	

خَرُوفْ

Sheep

Dub	Daal	د

دِبّ

Bear

Dheeb	Thaal	ذ

ذُئب

Wolf

Raccoon	Raa	

راكون

Raccoon

Zarafa	Zaa	زْ

زرافة

Giraffe

Sulahfat	Seen	س س

سلحفاة

Turtle

| Shimpanzee | Sheen | 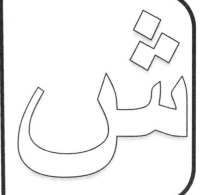 |

Chimpanzee

شمبانزي

Saqr	Saad	ص

Falcon

صقر

Difdae	Daad	ضْ

ضْفدَع

Frog

Taus	Taa	ط

طاووس

Peacock

Dhabey	Dha	

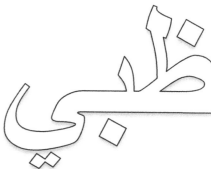

Fawn

Ocab	Ayn	ع

عقاب

Eagle

Ghazel	Ghayn	غَ

غَزال

Gazelle

Feel	Faa	فْ

فِيْل

Elephant

Qunfud	Qaaf	

قُنْفُذ

Hedgehog

Kalb	Kaaf	ك ك

كلب

Dog

Llama	Laam	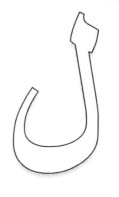

لاما

Llama

Maeiz	Meem	

Goat

ماعز

Namir	Nuun	

Tiger

نمر

Hudhud	Haa	هـ

Hoopoe

هد هد

| Watwat | Waaw | و |

وطواط

Bat

Yasuub	Yaa	ي

يعسوب

Dragonfly

Chapter 02:

Let's Color
The Arabic Numbers

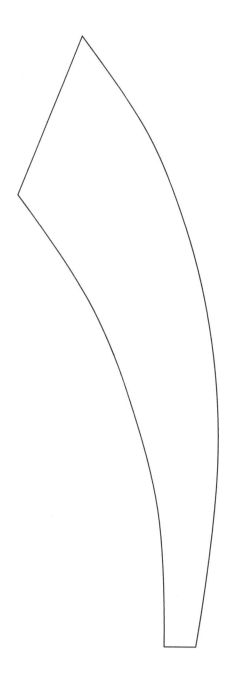

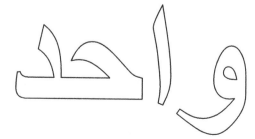

One

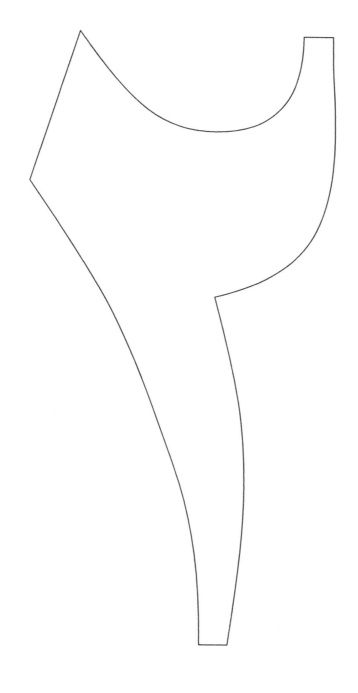

Two

اثنان

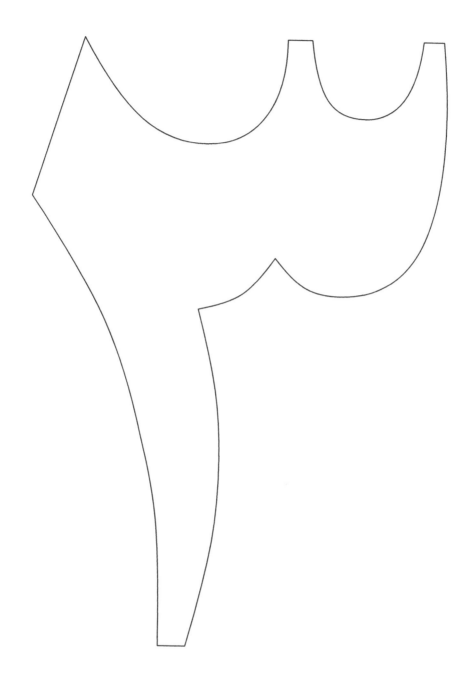

ثلاثة

Three

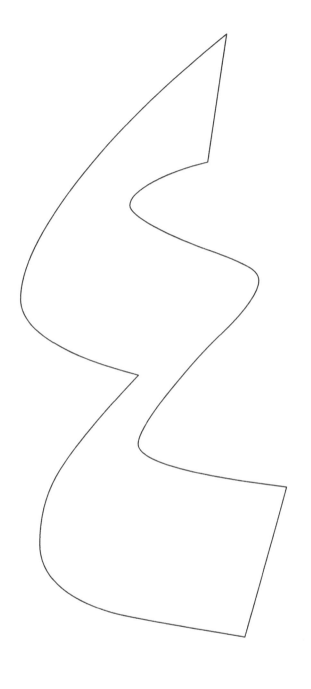

أَرْبَعة

Four

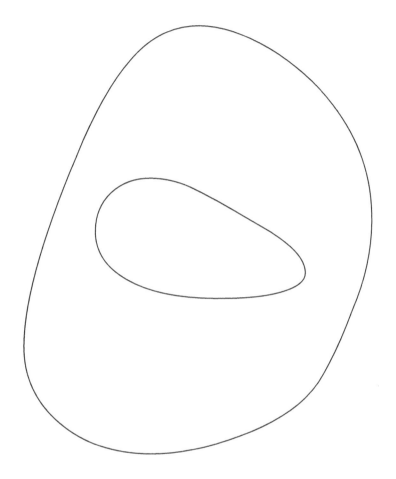

خَمْسة

Five

ستة

Six

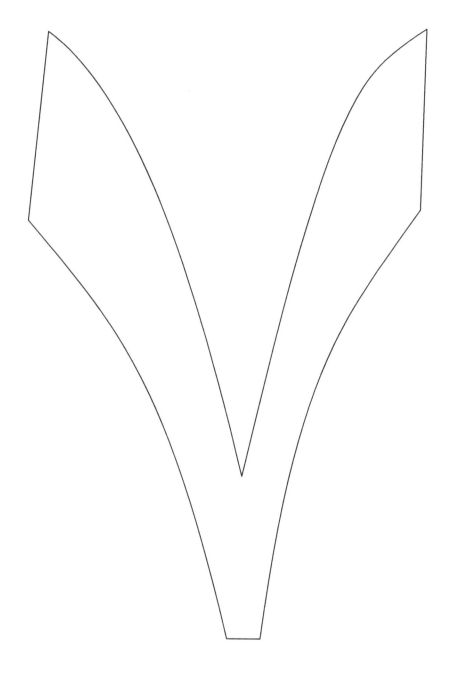

سبعة

Seven

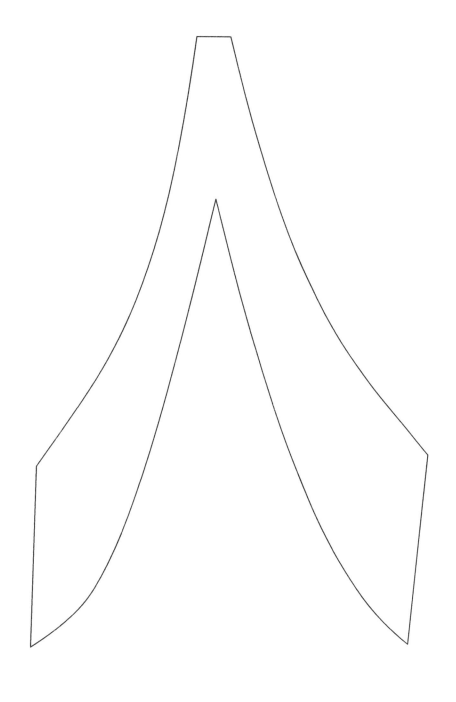

ثمانية

Eight

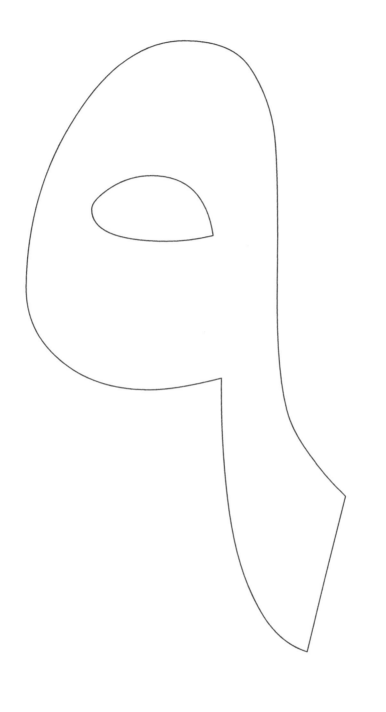

تسعة

Nine

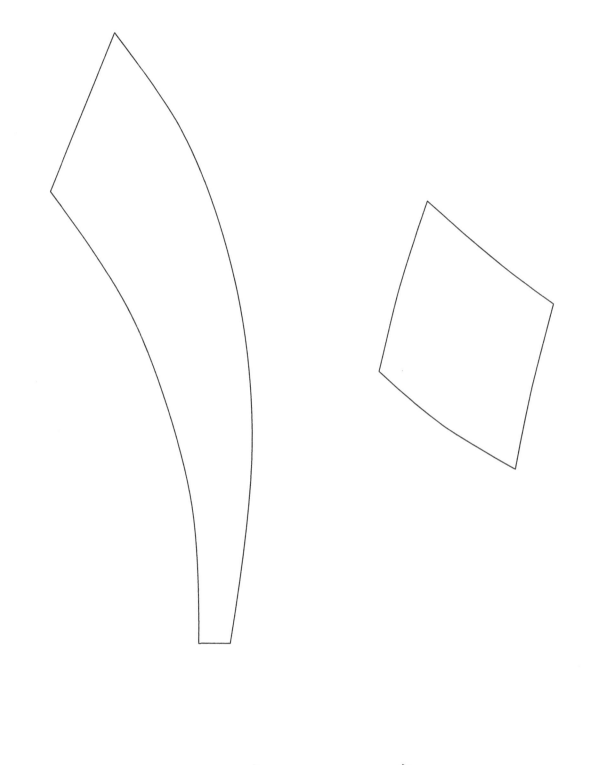

Ten

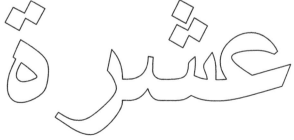

Certificate of
Achievement

Awarded to

....

Date: ....

Signed: ....

You are
Awesome

شهادة تقدير

تمنح هذه الشهادة إلى

....

تقديراً ....

الفصل ....

اسم المعلمة

توقيع

ختم
المدرسة

Made in the USA
Las Vegas, NV
30 June 2024

91689047R00050